Indian Rope Trick

For Alexandra —
Fellow - Spirit
in color
&
light —
Keep
Shining!

poems by
Prartho Sereno

BLUE LIGHT PRESS ◆ 1ST WORLD PUBLISHING

1st WORLD
PUBLISHING

SAN FRANCISCO ◆ FAIRFIELD ◆ DELHI

Winner of the 2018 Blue Light Book Award

Indian Rope Trick

Copyright ©2018 by Prartho Sereno

1ST WORLD LIBRARY
PO Box 2211
Fairfield, IA 52556
www.1stworldpublishing.com

BLUE LIGHT PRESS
www.bluelightpress.com
bluelightpress@aol.com

BOOK & COVER ART & DESIGN
Melanie Gendron
melaniegendron999@gmail.com

COVER ART
from the watercolor painting *Indian Rope Trick* by Prartho Sereno, 2018

AUTHOR PHOTO
Angelina Samadhi

FIRST EDITION

Library of Congress Control Number: 2018950597

ISBN 9781421838120

Acknowledgments

Grateful acknowledgement to the following publications in which these poems first appeared:

Bellevue Literary Review: "June Bugs"
Boomers Lit Magazine: "Oath of Omission"
Chattahoochee Review: "Right Now"
Comstock Review: "Gravitas" and "What Shape Sadness"
Dreaming at the Gates: "Sailing, Three Years Old"
Finding Home: Stories of Living in Marin: "California's Secret"
  (published as "Our Secret," an excerpt of which is carved at the
  entry of Homeward Bound, Novato, CA)
Marin Poetry Center Anthology, 2016, Water: "View from Canal du
  Rhône à Sète"
Marin Poetry Center Anthology, 2017, Getting the News: "Evidence"
Marin Poetry Center Anthology, 2018: "Indian Rope Trick"
Poem in Your Pocket/ Berkeley Public Library: "Willy at 92" and
  "Summers at Honeoye Lake"
Rattle: "A Few Questions Before We Go On"
San Diego Poetry Annual: "On the Train from Paris to Provence" and
  "Refusing Grace"
Singing the Feathers of Freedom, CPITS 2017 Anthology:
  "What the Child Knows"
Sixteen Rivers Press 2018 Anthology: "When the Aliens Come"
Spillway: "Scarlett's Secret"
Stone Canoe: "We Can Stop Asking"
West Marin Review: "The Dancing Cure" and
  "Emergency Lock-Down Drill"
When the Muse Calls: Poems for the Creative Life:
  "Poet in the City of Fear"

Heartfelt thanks to the many friends and poets who supported me in the creation of these poems, especially my students of the past twenty years (ages 6 to 93), my small but lionhearted poetry circle — Kosrof Chantikian and Catlyn Fendler, my submissions partner Karen Benke, and the Marin Poet Laureate Committee, created and guided by the vision of Dick Brown.

Thank you also to Diane Frank of Blue Light Press who believed in me and this project, my loony loving family, and my sweetheart, Dennis, who gets me to our place of worship every Sunday—barefoot at the National Seashore at Limantour Beach.

Also by Prartho Sereno

Poetry

Elephant Raga

Call from Paris

Causing a Stir: The Secret Lives & Loves of Kitchen Utensils

Garden Sutra (a chapbook)

Essays

Everyday Miracles: An A to Z Guide to the Simple Wonders of Life

Editor

Everyday Osho: 365 Daily Meditations for the Here & Now

Indian Rope Trick

To my brothers of body & soul
Gary, Sid, & Bodhi
for your splendidly weird & wonderful selves

and for the wake of silence you left
when you set sail
in your scattered fleet

Table of Contents

III

. . .there was a time when people could be astonished.

— David Von Drehle
"The Circus Leaves Town"
Time Magazine 5/15/17

*The rope must be thrown into the air
and defy the force of gravity,
while someone climbs it
and disappears.*

— Robert Elliot of the London Magic Circle
in his challenge to world magicians
to recreate the Indian Rope Trick

I

We Can Stop Asking

We can stop asking, because, really,
on the subcontinent of India anyway,
everybody knows where time goes:
down the Ganges. That's why the sick
and old go to die there, to slow
their breath to its muddy pulse.
And why mourners float miniature boats
from her banks, heaped with marigolds
making the river sob purple and orange.

And everybody at the Ganges knows
that time passes like smoke — a pungent furl
of nearly nothing, more delicate than silk.
We would like to sew a dress from it
and wear it to the wedding. We would like
to make a tent of it to carry on our backs.

But time is not a river or smoke.
It's more like the billow and sway
the smoke and river do. More like
the surge and swell of morning light —
a sneaker wave aimed for the shore,
a hunger in the water that wants us,
every last one of us, back at sea.

The First Rule

Multiply any number by nothing and you come up
with nothing. You could begin by counting the hairs
on your head or the snow flakes filling the pines.

You could start with a river, riotous with alligators,
a migratory cloud of monarchs, or a lone whale lost at sea.
You can wriggle your fingers toward the last known sum

or tunnel into the loam of minuses, where every
asset turns to loss. Marry whatever you've tallied
to zero, and the halls will be cleared of their streamers

and white paper bells. Your hands will be emptied
of rice. No bridal waltz, no ring bearer.
The groom won't turn up at the altar.

All will be as if it never was — brought back
to the weightless, the invisible. To the numinous
pull that yearns to arrive, to be counted.

My Daughter Falls in Love

Given that she came from nowhere
or as close to nowhere as I've been —
the dark ravine where love pitches us,
sometimes, if we're lucky . . .

And given her first rush forth —
that reverse disappearing act,
that bright burst of being. . .
Given these and the three days
it took for her name to fall
like a feather
from her father's mouth . . .

we expected the rustle
of wingbeats in the air
where she moved.
But to watch her fall now
from so high and land,
delicate as a raindrop
on the head of a pin,
is almost too much
for us to bear.

We are shot through again
with the ancient sorrow
that courses through love
with its flickering filaments of joy.

Wedding Poem

for B & S

I'm thinking about things that surrender:
pebbles dropped into water, willows that weep
in the wind, a seed pod broken open
by something wild waking inside.

I'm thinking of a man at the brink of 85
who looks over the front seat of the Honda
to ask about the passing years. *I forget,*
he says. Is life short? Or is it long?

He has at last said yes to his woman: his housemate
of 30 years, co-cook and bottlewash, co-planner
and schemer, co-riser-up from the muds
of disappointment. He admits when she's out
of the room that a long-lost voice cleared its throat
one day to whisper inside: Marry that woman.

And so the rumpus begins: the stirring up
of guest lists and soup. Brush-clearing teams
and tent teams, flower girls, bakers, and the indispensable
balloon squad. And all the flurry takes me back
to an old friend who said near his end, *I used to think*
nothing could touch me. Now . . . everything does.

I know, you're wondering how this stranger
got into Bodhi and Shakti's poem. Especially since
I've said nothing about the other surrender:

hers. Or the color she brings to all she touches —
the way she coaxes the unlikeliest among us
to blossom. Particularly our heads,
kaleidoscopically abloom in her crochet hats.

And I haven't gotten round to tell you
about the silence she keeps deep in her sleeves —
the lamp that was lit in her, alone at the Indian shrine.

And we haven't yet remembered how the two of them
were green with envy and plotted an ambush
on the holders of the forested lot next door . . .
Until the day they discovered the owners were them.

This wedding day is that kind of ambush — on the ones
we've been envying: ourselves. In the planning stages,
he kept saying over the phone: *After we all get married* . . .
Even corrected, he just went on: *Yes, yes, after we all*
get married… we can jump in the lake. Or skip back
singing at the top of our lungs. Or romp like peepers
leaping for spring.

Truth is, he is fixing to marry us all. Throughout his life —
the short and the long of it — he's always wanted to marry
the world. And now he can, thanks to the persistent
updraft, Shakti's warm breath of Yes at his back: Yes
everything can touch us now, and we will marry it all.

Gone

He slipped out while none of us was looking,
our chancellor emeritus of the back road.
Made his exit en route among strangers
and angels — his closest kin.

When the body arrived in the flashing red
hubbub of ER, it was already empty.
Empty as the night would be
with its owl sailing through it.

Empty as the morning with its pale
yellow light, and the breakfast nook
where he shuffled his kings and queens.

Each of us were left to make what sense of it
we could. But alone in our private precincts,
I don't think anybody could.

Right Now

It hasn't rained in this town for months,
but somewhere on the planet puddles
are mad with it, and in some otherwhere
it hangs like fishnets in the air.

Now, as with all nows, morning breaks somewhere —
cows are let out to graze and runaway colors return
to the cupboards. Somewhere the sun has just
vanished with a flash of green into the sea.

Right now a porter in Mumbai is asleep
on the cement at Victoria Station; India's pandemonium
of heat and colored light has opened her cool
dark mouth and taken him in.

In Guatemala, an old woman threads her needle
in the shade of the volcano as it makes its daily
slide across the *lago*. In Istanbul, a grief-stricken
man stops to sing out in the streets.

Right now on this planet an olive is midair
in its fall from the tree, a moonflower closes
on its trellis, and a pale pomegranate root
breaks through its seed.

Somewhere an old man falls down the stairs,
the lost ring is found in the drawer where everyone
looked a hundred times, and a veil
has been lifted from eyes.

Somewhere on this bright ball, women come home
with jugs of water on their heads, a family's only
camel dies in the dust, and a band of neighbors
manages to put out the fire.

Whales breach, elephants kneel to drink,
and countless parrots drop a single
bright feather — all of them aflutter now
together in our sky.

View from Canal du Rhône à Sète

Half way round the world, here too,
workers gather in the predawn dark.
They warm their hands around coffee
and talk up the sun who flings out her colors
like a silk merchant opening shop. Here too,
the herons and gulls leap into the morning,
the ducks grump and grumble before
shoving off. Here too, the doves swoop into
the willow's honeycomb of early light.

As for us, we untie our moorings and begin.
Roll past well-kept craft and sunken ones;
our imaginations roam the storied banks.

And here's the old fisherman, come
to resume his post — beside the stone pilings
where the fish jump high. When this
old fisherman dies, I think, another
will come to take his place. Just like
the egrets — there is always one
where one ought to be. You don't notice
the dying. All you see is a river of egrets
and fishermen. Rivers of old women
and children, with no gap. Like the water
on its way to the sea.

On the Train from Paris to Provence

Who am I to her — that young woman who
carries my name, half a lifetime ago, on a train?
She's pulling out of Rome, making poems
about the ruins. Me, I have Paris to leave —
other ruins (*mes cheveux blancs*). She travels
with her Italian husband who complains
that her sandals lack grace, that she always wants
the high-priced sit-down table at cafes.

She rarely thinks of me. Never, really,
except in the generic sense: yoga, dental floss,
broccoli. And maybe that one time as a child
when squinting through fever she found
an old crone looking out from the mirror.

But she never thinks of me the way I do her. She can't
imagine herself a white-haired woman leaving Paris —
gray sky, new man even older than she. He writes
postcards beside her as the city melts away
and the world without warning goes green.

It will stay unrequited, my love for her,
the bittersweet of it. Still, I wonder
if something of this moment comes to her,
light as a moth, as the car rocks and rolls
away from Rome. Maybe it feels as if the train
has briefly entered a patch of tenderness
where something old awakens in her
and hums a childhood song.

Another Life

In another life I was a hermit.
A mountain man,
my only company the crows.
They shared my hungers
and kept my secrets.
They scrubbed the afternoons
with their cries.

Passersby kept their distance.
Not that anyone could blame them —
my gnarly face and deep-set eyes
brimming with bad weather.

How could they know
such a rag of a body
could carry a heart
spun of glass?

There was a girl in the village,
warm as an oil lamp, eyes brown
as rain-drenched dirt.

But she never came to know
my love — no matter how many notes
I sent from the hills,
in the mouths of crows.

What Shape Sadness?

Something like a teacup, I think.
Bone-thin and hollow —
a waiting.

Sadness yearns
for wind-raked beaches
and doors shook from their hinges.
The sound of horses' hooves,
the smell of rain.

She is the one you hear sobbing
in the basilica of your bones —
her roof beams high, her vestibule
mopped and empty.

Sadness is the beautiful
nameless thing the dying friend
brings through the door,
the baritone warmth of his body
leaning on yours.

King Tides

There's a calm before the storm
of making love,
before we pull down the moon
that pulls in the flood. Before
the levies and dikes go under,
everything on the verge swept in.

Here comes the ramshackle
raft of my life. There goes
my childhood, my melancholy teens.
There go years on the payroll,
tattered travelogues, pacts
between me and the papered walls.

Here come the forest paths
and the sandstone cliffs.
Here comes the jasmine-dense air.

There's the sunlight and the fire
and the filagree of steam
that rises from morning.
Now the city lights and the flashing
quicksilver sea.

And isn't that us, watching
from the hill as the mystery
makes her entrance
and takes up the crown?

Threading the Beads

The great swan on the wing —
flight of the alone to the alone.
                                    — zen

1.   You are a child when you first slip
        through a tear in the ruckus, down
        the rocky banks to the lake
        where your name turns to mist
        and the silence sidles up
        to unlatch the trapdoor of the world.

        When you least expect it, she's there again —
        as a beggar at the curb giving you a glimpse
        of the unmarred face behind her face.

        Evidence continues to build: the whale
        breaches when no one else is there. You're
        alone on the shore when the black swan swims
        to your feet. The child, delirious with fever,
        mutters clues in an octave only you can hear.

        You will have to bear these on your own,
        without corroboration, even those
        who want to believe   never quite will.

2.   Meanwhile, the ordinary will continue its rounds:
        a fleet of cloud-ships plows the predawn sky.

        You arrange the pears in a basket,
        fill the pot with cream.

        The stainless bowl rings
        as you take it from the shelf.

You carry on even though the bottomless
has taken hold and you know

from now on you can only wander
like a Lakota Heyoka — backwards.

3.   This is what it is to love the Leavers:
Night fills with echoes,
darkness rolls out from day.
You can't stop dreaming

of the waterways lacing
the Oleander Palace,
how you lived there once
when your soul took the shape
of a long-legged, blue-beaked bird.

Stop the Wheel

How is it that on this
the first day of summer
the sun has already packed
her bags and hailed a cab
toward winter?

Stop the wheel!
is what the grandfather
kept yelling in the story
my friend told so often
it became my own —
a moment that has made me.

We are seven
and the grandfather
is dying as we bump along
in the bullock cart
on India's rutted roads.
The old man burns
with fever, the boy dizzy
with question: *what*

does the grandfather want
of this overgrazed field?
why doesn't the grandmother
stop driving the bull?

The spinning ferocious,
the doctor impossibly far.
The wheel uncompromising —
rolling along, as if that's all
it was meant to do.

Sid's Last Stroke

Being that the gale blew in on the left, his wits
had no choice but to migrate right. Which is to say
he's boarded up the sea shanty of reason and
shoved off — furiously battening down his schooner
as it cuts the waves. She, meanwhile,
moves herself to the living room, writes emails
from the folding table, sleeps on the couch
beside the rented hospital bed that he steers out
each night, frantically reprimanding his crew.

Every now and then he's back at harbor. Every now
and then, she says, he's himself again. He doesn't
mistake her for an ex-lover or ex-wife. He doesn't call
for the head nurse or manager of this inhospitable inn.
He puts aside the tedium of rerouting his vessel
around the serpentine sorrows. He falls in
behind those salt-blue eyes, uses her name,
asks for her hand, wants to know
what she needs to do before she dies.

He's speaking in metaphor, the social worker
has pulled her aside to say. And a bit sternly:
Enter it. Stop trying to bring him back.
And so she does what she can — teeters out
onto the creaky dock and kisses her handsome sailor.
She says fare-thee-well in every language she knows,
undoes the mooring, and gives the bow a shove —
knowing well that from the ship's-eye-view
she'll only get smaller, no matter how largely
she waves. Smaller and smaller until the day
when the slightest breeze will blow her away.

Indian Rope Trick

It's the mystery's favorite trick: weaving
the intricate rope of someone's life, then
lifting it for them to climb and somewhere
near the top . . . disappear.

Two weeks ago my brother told me
he'd shot nine holes. Pain was lousy, he said,
but went on to try out punchlines he'd been
practicing for his meeting with the Maker.

I'm not afraid to die, he said
with that curious wonder he had
since the diagnosis. But this time
he added he had no regrets.
None worth counting, anyway.

I'd taken my phone on my walk and was talking
to him from the mountain, at the level of ravens
and hawks. He'd had a wonderful life, he said,
which caused the rope of it to rise and grow taut
so we could see it in all its color: There in his yellow

cowboy pajamas with his champion Alaskan yoyo.
There in the glow of his cherry-bomb days.
There at the helm of the stolen tractor on a joyride
over the golf club greens. And look: now he's doing

figure eights on his forklift in the basement of Kodak.
Now he's blasting off, bottle-rocket-style, to
international VP. See him there in Paris and Philly?
See him adrift on South Carolina's inlet seas?

Here come the whole buzzing swarm
of friends drawn in by the honey of his ease.
Ah. . . we seem to have followed that rope
right up through the clouds.

I couldn't have asked for more, he said.
And his exhale filled the valley
so the hawks lifted up on the rising air.
And we said goodbye.

II

Seeing Things

Look, there's Jerry at the fish counter,
climbed up out of his depression and flown in
from San Francisco, just to trip by as if
he didn't see me. Ah, but that's not Jerry, is it?
And that's not Lois either. Or Debbi's mother,
brightly confused, back from the dead. But that
wasn't quite what I meant by seeing things.

I meant more like the dream where your newborn
daughter steps through a curtain of saris,
suddenly grown, and the vision of what's to come
flies off the wheel to deep-dive inside.

But that's not exactly what I mean either.
I'm talking something like that dazzling red
honeymoon star, the chrysanthemum of fire
that reeled down toward our car as we drove
through the Poconos on our wedding night.
Sky torn open, burnt through with hope
and oncoming sorrow, as we stood
at the frayed edge of the world.

Or maybe this is what I'm trying to say:
On our drive to their birthplace I counsel
the born-out-of-wedlock twins about the way time
can get bunched up, how the past and the future
might suddenly end up in the same spot.
But they're good in math and look skeptical;
we skip stones over it before reluctantly
heading to that big red X:

You Were Born Here, I tell them. This
is the avenue of your first one hundred days.

Broken-beer-bottle rivulets, plastic bags
darting in the wind. Unzip your memories,
I say, your teenage-boy hearts; sniff deep . . .
as we stop at the crosswalk for this man

burrowed into his hooded sweatshirt with his
brown paper bag, who turns up ever so briefly
his face, his war-torn, revolving-door-prisoner,
I-used-to-know-you, Mrs. Sereno, when-I-came-
in-the-night-to-kiss-your-sweet-daughter, his
turned-away-so-quickly-now-but-the-afterimage-
burning, his oh-my-god-that-was-your-father,
your never-known-and-perhaps-never-will,
your deeply-lost father's face.

Oath of Omission

This time I'm going to leave out the part
that sneaks onto the cottage roof to listen in
on the trees. I won't bother with the popsicle truck
that limped down the tarred and pebbled road,
or how, at dinner, my brothers got me to turn my head
so they could slide their helping of cow's tongue
on my plate. I won't wax on about the possum
that perched on the deck-rail with saffron moons
for eyes or how easy it is to empty your heart
at the edge of a lake. I won't give away the secrets
the poplars tell in their seances or what willows
laugh about on summer nights.

I'll keep quiet on the year that floated out from under us
like a phantom ship and the map it scratched in the sand,
washed out before anybody could read it. Maybe we'll think
about that one day, but today let's leave it out — along with
the holy water the altarboy-paperboy brought in a jelly jar
for my mother. He told her it could cure a host of ills,
from poison ivy to the loss of faith. She laughed a bit
as she closed the door, put the jar up beside the pickles
and jams, but she used it, in earnest, when my father got sick.

No, we won't go into all that. The map is long-gone
and whatever was left of the holy water has surely
gone back into air.   We'll leave this poem
with all its holes — a breezeway, a windswept hollow,
a nearly imperceptible ripple, as close
as we can get to nothing at all.

Tornado, Sisters

The three of us on the back porch, bowls slopped
with meatballs and spaghetti, our weeping

cups of lemonade. Each of us on the verge
of bloom, a tilt-a-whirl of hanker, a somersault of want.

Out in the yard — bachelor buttons and black-eyed
Susans, nightshirts and pillow sacks flapping on the line.

When from out of the heat-heavy air — out beyond
the hedgerow — a small tornado spins itself, seductive

as the devil's fishline. It comes for us and tosses
our hair, like we're cruising in a Cadillac.

It guzzles twigs as it careens across the field.
Tiny as tornados go, but drunker than a sailor.

Our mother — a funnel of worry in a calico apron —
snatches up the stainless serving bowl

with its fallen masts of wooden spoons
and shouts for us to come. But we stay
                    wonderstruck

at the edge of that oncoming dark — three still points
at the center of the wind-wild world.

Twelfth Day of Rain

For nearly two weeks —
her uncles grumbling
in the counting room —
the sky has been giving away
the family jewels.

For us down here
it's all splurge: starlings
muck about in puddles,
sidewalks sing in Cantonese,
the mushrooms raise their radiant
saucer-shaped heads.

Even the rocks soften in her hands.
The stone-faced mountain
has broken into sobs.

February in Maine

Babies in the house, mud-caked
bucket on the table — our modest harvest
of potatoes and beets. I light the fire,
stir the pot. The kitchen fills with smells
of burnt sugar and apple. It's February
and Maine — for most of a month the sun
won't quite look our way. She'll dress in gauzy
layers — a visitant with a distant gaze.
She'll barely skim the ridge of pine.
Today I'll bake bread, knead the dough
like a dogged memory. I'll check on
the chickens, start a batch of yogurt. The girls
will ride my body through the dust motes
that glint in doorways. I'll stagger
beneath the happy weight.
Later they will cry — tears big
and silvery as ice cubes. We'll shiver together
like we did in the birthing rooms.
We won't hold back.

White Mountains

Something of me is still
there on the frozen field.
Parka and sneakers,
white clouds of my breath.
The ship of my life sunk
beneath the wooded rise.

No more kitchen, no more
mountain man, no more
glowing hearth. This
is where I come to know
what the moon must feel.
How close and empty the stars.

This is when the night splinters
into starlings to flap and murmurate
through me. Their dark wings whisper
of another world I long to reach,
but they leave no footpath
in the sky.

Poem in Defiance of Gravity

I keep telling myself it's time to come down,
surrender to the wiles of the good old US of A —
its mastercards, metering lights, and ziplock bags.
Replant my roots in the California dirt
that gives us free-range eggs and gluten-free bread.
But I can't stop this extravagant wanting
to wing my way back to the fragrances and stinks

of India — belch of rickshaw, clang of cowbell,
dogs and chickens digging through the trash.
My heart wants to drift again with the riverferns.
To float between banks slathered in saris
spread out to dry. I ache for the songs of women
doing laundry, chewing the daylight, spitting out pan.

I want to get back to the afternoon lull — teakettles
on rolling carts, heady with cardamom and clove.
To cross the threshold that opens wherever
the midday heat strikes you down — most likely
on the stone bench under the almond tree
with its cavalcade of beetles in emerald cloaks.

O give my eyes back to the paradise bird
and its blue-green long-tailed loops.
Lend my ears once more to the one
who sings from deep in the bamboos —
hidden from the eye, but with a call
trained straight for the heart.

Uncle Joe & the Blizzard of '76

Uncle Joe was an iceman, a snowglobe
of a man, his body a blur of wonder.
His was a white hunger, a yearning
for the cold that might glaze the world,
for the day he might walk on water.

He was blessed with the Blizzard of '76.
Speechless in his snowshoes
he plodded into the stunned city
and came back changed. He'd try
to talk about what met him there,
but could never finish the sentence.

All his life he told whoever'd listen
his greatest wish was to be taken:

When those snow-colored saucers come —
that graceful host of fallen moons,
*   give them my address.*

Greg, Shoveling

Today, through the backlit
pixilated window on my desk,
I see my brother digging out.

The sky-tracks above Niagara
have slipped out from under
the hi-speed commuter train
as it barreled down from the Pole,
and its sleepy cargo of snow gods
have dumped their icy disgruntlements
all over Buffalo.

From the California Coast
I dial my periscope to see him —
a dark figure bent over
his shovel, cutting a grotto
into the light.

He is valiant, as always.
But what chance has this
big-handed barrel-bodied
bear of a man
against the cold
white
mystery?

Ingrid

All she wants is a dog — an animal
the color of unpeeled potatoes.

She wants a confidante who believes
in the tip of his nose, who stakes it all

on the fickle counsels of the wind.
All she wants is a fur-feathered friend

with a plum for a heart. To hold
that quiver of wilderness and want

before letting it go — leaves flying up
like castaway birds.

Willy at 92

Up before dawn so she won't have to rush,
Willy gives herself to the little things.

Nowadays everybody wants big things,
she says. *Noisy things.*

But she likes the quiet part of the day —
when it starts to get dark and she lights the fire.

A month ago she lost her spaniel Beauregard
and misses their chats.

What did you talk about? I ask.
Oh, whatever was happening right then . . .

He was very here and now.

Scarlett's Secret

Her mother sang the nights away in Vaudeville,
slept late in the mornings, spent hazy, ruby-
lipped hours in the mirror. Until one morning
the daughter made a pact with her own legs

so they gave way beneath her. She became a perfect
rag-doll for her mother to take up in arms,
pass through London's streets, legs sloshing,
down a bucket-brigade of doctors. But still

the fire raged. At last one hazarded polio
and all were strangely relieved; the mother
continued to lift her delicate angel
over a year of books and bedroom light.

And then, the equally sudden cure: One day
the daughter stood and walked back to the world.

California's Secret

By early afternoon we're haunted again;
all of us a little bit lonesome
for what we left behind when we packed up
the VW or the station wagon.
Or maybe we just grabbed hands and ran —
headlong into the deep end of America's Dream.

Now we are in it together, awash
in the salt water of our well-kept secret:
Our bodies ache — for lightning bugs
and summer rain, fresh peeled cactus
and the smell of adobe walls.
Our daydreams are scored with snow against windows
or a chorus of parrots in the tamarind trees.

Even California's native son gets homesick,
wishes he could walk through the belled door
of the corner store or take the slow train home.
Even the Miwok sighs with the sun's daily slide
toward its hills of gold, nostalgic for the sound
of his own footfalls on the soft and giving ground.

The Perfection of 9

After the requisite dinosaurs,
monsters and mummies,
my brother Greg was swept away
by the 9 tables. He wrote them
in furious columns for most of a year —
page after delirious page —
until his passions turned to fire and
he used them for kindling, nearly
burning us all down. But by then

9's mysteries had gotten into him —
a permutation of French doors,
each framed by two digits that eerily,
unfailingly, added to 9: 8 & 1, 7 & 2,
6 & 3, 5 & 4. After that, his eyes
were like mirrored entries, reflecting
themselves back and forth through
the calculable universe. It's not so
easy casting out nines.

What else measures up? Seven
with its 7 wonders and its 7 deadly sins?
Well-heeled 5 in his wide-brimmed hat?
One is indisputably upright, 3 and 8
have their corpulent charms. 4 is a tulip
in the garden of digits. But 9, that needle
with a lopsided eye, is a portal so
generous you can step right through,
where even your camel might pass.

refusing grace

sometimes
all you're given
for days
are tears
which you can
of course
refuse
you can
keep repairing
the levees
you can
hole up
in the cobwebs
of your skull
you can
refuse
the weeping
which only
wants to float you
like alice
out the door

what matters

sun-bleached bones
and the changing colors of the sea

beetles and brooms
bicycles and pencils

animals with thumping hearts
and working brains

saturday
with its sloppy edges
morning
with its stockinged feet

november
because it's gray
and difficult

young girls' hair
and fishlines in the air
because their feelings for the wind
are so transparent
and true

Poet in the City of Fear

The only dancers in the City of Fear
are wooden. They clunk along the broken
streets, pointing the way with their elbows.

The city builders are crazed — haphazard
scaffolding, wrecking balls and cranes.
Their teetering towers of mirrored glass.

The trees in the city are thronged with monkeys,
air a smudge of smoke and ash;
brown rivers bob with debris.

The only poet in the City of Fear
is dumb and nearly blind. He sleeps
among the rubble, but sometimes

a dusty hum rolls out of him, down the hill.
There's another world, you can almost
hear it say. *Beyond the wall and muddy river.*

*It's a land of flow and flutter, of dragon fruit
and long-tailed birds. Wild things grow up from
the ground. Things can flower there — even words.*

Notes from the Field

Steps have to be followed, but sometimes
they can wonder away from you.
— from a student essay

And so we begin. Well, not exactly we, more like me
all by myself, taking my first step onto the field.
Blindfolded. If you listen to *Science Friday*, you know

where this is leading. It's the same for everybody,
the researcher proclaimed this morning, giddy
with a certainty yet unknown to science: Blindfold

any person and aim her into an expanse of grass.
Soon enough she'll be walking in circles. *Yes!*
the researcher says with relish: *Everyone.*

In decades of trials on the vast and motley they've yet
to find an exception. He's dizzy with it: our profound
inability to walk a line. And I'm so there with him

in that dizzy. Well, not exactly there, of course,
but here where we started. And not exactly we
(I remind myself) but me in my little quorum of one.

But I'm procrastinating. Steps have to be followed.
Blindfolded. Without you. One foot at a time, though
I'm pretty sure they've already started to wonder away.

III

Evidence

The the sun rides in on its palanquin of bees

Prayers bend round us like light

Day's smells shiver up like moths

And look: flowers of wind / rivers of sky

See how the cow's eye and the hedgehog's nose
are wet with it

How the lilac bends and the stones go still for it

Have faith in this our late-day mudslide of shadow

Death carries us in her mouth — softly
as if we were her own

Feel of the Cloth

The emperor wanted to believe
the itinerant tailors — that the robe they'd
made for him had been woven of light.

Which, of course, it was.
Of sunlight and air.
His heartbeat quickened as they
pointed out the iridescent beads of dew
and delicate taffeta of fog,
the pale blue moonglow trim.

The emperor wanted to hear
the whisper of wingbeats as he
fingered the cloth, to smell
the sweet decay of the forest floor.

And so he did. As he dove head-first
into that glorious garment he heard
and smelled uncountable things.
It was like nothing, he said
when he regained his wits, like nothing

he'd ever put on. Like wearing a cloud.
Or a breeze. It's not of this world,
he said to the tailors, who nodded
and smiled . . . Which, come to think of it,
was their only lie. For this world

was precisely what they used for their warp,
our commonest threads their woof.

When the Aliens Come

When those radiant mango-eyed beings
light down at last on the wheat fields
and ball parks of our planet, it won't be

to speak with our leaders; they won't ask
to be taken to the summit or talk about
trade. They will come for the trees.

They'll ask to be brought to the shade
of banyans and old-growth redwoods.
To the ancient cedars of Lebanon.

They will come to sit with the elders.
To sink their feet into the earth
and drink with them. They will come

for the understory, to listen for the urgencies
that stir the longing and break the seed.
They'll want to learn the art of standing

firm in two worlds — to share secrets
with mushrooms and larvae while
holding a bird in the palm of your hand.

Theirs will not be to puzzle over gravity
or strategies for keeping boots on the ground.
They will come for the other law —

the upward surge, the inexorable craving
for starlight — and dark matter, that melancholy
chord that braids through and through.

What We Lost, Near the Beginning

Near the beginning,
before cobblestones and sidewalks.
Before street lamps, headlights,
and neon signs — there was more mud.
                    More stars.

Every tree and rock along the footpath
bore its own inimitable pull.
You could feel your way through the world
                with your eyes closed.

There was more dying, to be among.
Death was like family — you knew the lines
of her forehead, the scent
of her breath. You slept and woke
to her familiar thrum in the hills.

Everyone's thoughts were round
and moved like the planets, in circles.
God was a kind of circle
                only less precise:

sometimes she was a bird,
                sometimes the moon,
sometimes she looked out
from your mother's face.

Her angels were legion
and in plain sight —
                they rose in flocks
at the slightest footfall,
excitedly stirring the air.

Allotted Wonders

Made to chose one among the uncountable
we'll pass on our cross-country drive,
he goes for the grandest — to see
what the Colorado River has chiseled
into the layered eons — a stop
three quarters of the way.

He's pretzeled and unpretzeled
his 87-year-old body into and out of
the Honda's back seat for over 2200 miles
when we finally leave the highway
for juniper and sage. We're nearing the mark,
and somehow this makes him nervous.
Oh no! he leans up to whisper,
. . . *what if I'm disappointed?*

Think of it this way, I say, smiling
at the rearview, *it's half a day out of the car.*

At last we're trudging together, up
the little incline from the parking lot
when without warning the Earth
bares her sacred heart.

We're in the vestibule of a dug-out
cathedral, vaulted deep instead of high,
spilling with silence —
the only thing to survive the depths.

At last he's face to face with it,
and I should have been prepared.
I've seen him buckle under lesser things:
He breaks for sparrows, weeps
when we pass the corn at picnics.

Still, I stagger as I watch him
stumble backwards, recoiled
by his own laughter. And just
as quickly now, he's washed away
in a choking sea of sobs, which
is where I meet my own allotment —
going down with him
for the third time.

A Few Questions Before We Go On

Who gathered the straw and the twigs?
Who wove the nest and laid the egg
of this world? What patient one sat
and warmed it till it broke out in octopus
and chickadee, walrus and snake?

Who came up with all the comings and goings?
The breathing and eating. Sleeping
and waking. Who conjured the laugh?

Who thought up sex and where
we drop when we fall in?
Who dreamed the river of tears?

Who charmed the embryo's polliwog body
to flower into elbows and ears?
Who jolted the heart to throb?
Who thought up growing old?

What melancholic dramatist chose loss
for every scene — tragic, comic, slice-of-life?
And who is it that can't stop humming
as she sweeps up the stardust backstage?

Emergency Lock-Down Drill

Yesterday the third graders and I were writing about clouds
when it was announced that the Emergency Lock-Down Drill
was about to begin, during which we were to run and hide,
to find a place — behind the teacher's desk or under the oversized
cushions in the reading corner — where we could disappear.
Then the three shrill bursts, and the teacher raced to lock the door,
pull the blinds, douse the lights, all the while reminding us . . .
this teacher with a plum-blossom face, voice of a faraway cloud . . .
she told us to, please, stay still as stones, as if nobody were here.
And, as best we could, we did. Me, crouched next to the sink,
under the paper towel dispenser, the principal's commander-in-chief
voice oozing in through the PA. If someone dangerous were
running through the halls, he said, he should not be able
to see you. And so we sank deeper into the thickening dark,
trying to be small, but leaking out all over, at the edges of things.

Piano

It's been five sad years
since the silence fell next door,
since the neighbors' thirteen-year-old boy
was found in the kitchen
and taken away by the EMTs.

But now, behind the half-open upstairs
window, someone begins again
at the piano.

One stark note   after another.
As if a child   is practicing   scales:

        three parts   hesitation
one part   plunge.

I'm eating my lunch in the garden —
soup and lettuce, last night's fish.
The book whose plot can't hold me
lies open in my lap, when, after a gap
that seems to signal the recital's end,

the instrument   somehow
catches its breath and through
its hundred vocal chords sets loose
a winged thing — a music deep and holy,
as if every c-minor, b-flat, g-sharp —
every chord — has been summoned
to sound again.

As if the grief-knot has come
undone and love has been freed
to pour down again
over us and our parched gardens
like summer rain.

The Dancing Cure

Find your way back
to the cabin. Open
the doors, front
and back. Open
the windows, call in
the wind. Dance
till your bones clack
like bamboo.
Stir the soupy air
with your arms
and legs. Be like
the second-grade girl
in her poem about
the place of gold inside —
when she got there
she said she
dropped all her angers.

Gravitas

The sky is always falling.

But what drops in November
carries weight: nuts and leaves,
needles and seeds, the coarse
and tumbled lament of geese.

And in the afterglow, the silence
that falls on the fields.

The world has always longed
to take back the sky.
This is what Einstein and his friends
always miss when it comes to gravity.

With hunger for its root
and a homesick heart, gravity
is one of the names for love.

Summers at Honeoye Lake

Who would have thought a star
could get loose like that

like a wiggly tooth
and fall

that we could lie on the grass
at the edge of the lake and watch

the bonfire flirt
with the flaxen glow of fireflies

until a few wind-struck stars
got so stirred with envy

they'd let go
and somersault down

assuring us that the cold
grip of night

was not as unrelenting
or unforgiving
       as it seemed

What the Child Knows

The smell of sorrow — how it follows
a mother from room to room, redolent
of rutabaga and boiled cabbage,
windows dripping from the inside.

The child speaks a thousand tongues —
eye-blink, thunderhead, blackbird.
She understands hanker and itch, knows
when the shoe will drop and why
the bird must fly.

The child is privy to the blessing
of overcast skies, the nobility of grass.
She understands that praying goes better
in fallow fields, on your hands and knees.
At mushroom-level where the angels hide —
coaxing out blackberries, crocheting
their skeins of Queen Anne's lace.

Sailing, Three Years Old

I don't remember what it was that got me
up from bed to float in my pajamas
down the upstairs hallway to the window —
the leaded one with beveled glass
that scattered daylight
on the hardwood floor.

But I do remember the jump
through that window — out into the stars
where I sailed, briefly held, before
drifting down to the gravel below.

I loved the weightless part, but also
coming back into the shapes and smells
of the earth — hedges and rooftops,
the pile of neighborkids' bikes
heaped where they'd been dropped.
Crunch of stones beneath my feet.

I loved the dome of loneliness
I drifted through, a private observatory
for looking in on the world, which was,
for this little while, mine.

Then I took the stairs back up (*who knows
how? surely the doors were locked*)
and got into bed. I did this every night
for weeks on end, and nobody ever noticed.

Wish

Against all spell-casting wisdom, my sweetheart
blows out 74 candles and spills his wish:
To be young again, he says, looking into the trees.
And in through the mail slot between us
flies a piece of folded light, his answer
scribbled there in disappearing ink.
Yes, it says, even as it fades. *Soon enough . . .*

But first you will have to go back
to what the Hindu scholar nicknamed
the Forgettery, or what the three-year-old twin
urged his brother to remember as they talked
in the back seat of the Honda. *Remember
the Changey Thing?* he asked.
*After we go into the Changey Thing,
we get new shoes and a new back yard.
There'll be a different mother . . . Remember
that Changey Thing?*

But almost nobody remembers that turn
in the road, not even your own twin,
freshly sent forth,
so it's useless to bring it up.

June Bugs

As a child you found what was left
of them — exoskeletons clinging
to the bark of trees. Perfect
as anything. Perfect fit
for a child's hand. Perfectly empty,
perfectly whole. Bodies so
effortlessly slipped from

they looked like paper lanterns
or little wooden boats, scoured
and dry-docked for the winter.

It was tempting to think of them
as ghosts, but they're just
the opposite.

Not the part set free, but the part
swept clean — abandoned latticework cabins,
open to wind and rain.

Such meticulous tenants, those
June bugs. No one is as good
at leaving their bodies as they.

Last Words

The master lay dying
and his disciples gathered round
to plead, *Master! We're not ready.*
Please don't go.

To which the Old One laughed
and gazing through waning-moon eyes
replied: *Don't be ridiculous.*
Where would I go?

About the Author

Prartho Sereno is author of three previous poetry collections, including *Elephant Raga, Call from Paris*, and *Causing a Stir: The Secret Lives & Loves of Kitchen Utensils* (illustrated by the author). She served as Poet Laureate of Marin County, California, 2015—2017, has an MFA in Creative Writing from Syracuse University, and was awarded a Radio Disney Super Teacher Award for her 19-years' work as a California Poet in the Schools.

Prartho's poems are informed by many years living in a meditation community in India, but she also credits excursions into other "art forms:" counseling psychologist, mother of two, vegetarian cook, meditation instructor at Cornell University, book illustrator, and amateur singer-songwriter. Her life's ambition is to be a tour guide of the as-yet-unimagined, a tender of life's creative fires.

She lives a little north of the Golden Gate Bridge with a sweet man who takes her rowing on the bay.

CJR+

CPSIA information can be obtained
at www.ICGtesting.com
Printed in the USA
FSHW02n2228260918
52342FS